James P. Averill

Fort Meigs

A condensed History of the most important Military Point in the

Northwest

James P. Averill

Fort Meigs
A condensed History of the most important Military Point in the Northwest

ISBN/EAN: 9783337190941

Printed in Europe, USA, Canada, Australia, Japan

Cover: Foto ©ninafisch / pixelio.de

More available books at **www.hansebooks.com**

Most Important Military Point in the Northwest,

——TOGETHER WITH——

Scenes and Incidents connected with the Sieges of 1813,

——AND——

A Minute Description of the Old Fort and its Surroundings, as they now Appear.

———

JAMES P. AVERILL.

- - ◆ -

TOLEDO, OHIO:
BLADE PRINTING AND PAPER CO.
1886.

BIRD'S-EYE VIEW OF FT. MEIGS, FROM THE NORTH.

THE MAUMEE RIVER.

UP THE VALLEY FROM THE FORT. BATTLE-FIELD OF FALLEN TIMBERS IN THE DISTANCE.

THE MAUMEE RIVER (or "Miami of the Lake," as it was called during the war of 1812), was known by the Wyandotte Indians as "Cagh-a-ren-du-te," or "Standing Rock river," named from an elevated rock located in the middle of the stream, about a mile above the present town of Waterville, called by the French, "Roch de Boeuf." The Shawanoese (pronounced Sha-wa-no) named the stream the "Ot-ta-wa-sepe," or Ottawa river. The Ottawas had several towns on the river as late as 1812, on the rapids above Ft. Meigs, and also along Maumee Bay and the lake shore. The name "Maumee" is claimed by some writers to be a corruption of that given it by the French in the seventeenth century — "Au Miami;" it is authentically stated, however, that for centuries prior to this the beautiful stream had been known by the Indians who had retained possession of it despite the efforts of contending tribes, as "Mau-mee" — "Mother of Waters." It is a well-known fact that the Indians who lingered here to the last, loth to depart, fondly spoke of it as the "Maumee," the appropriate name which it will always hereafter retain. It is formed by a junction of the St. Joseph and St. Marys rivers at Ft. Wayne, Ind., runs in a northeasterly direction and empties into Lake Erie; its principal branch is the Auglaize, which joins it at Defiance. It is navigable for large boats as far as Ft. Meigs, immediately above the town of Perrysburg, on the right bank, and from this point, for many miles above, the stream is a succession of rapids, and its bed limestone rock.

ACROSS THE RIVER FROM THE FORT, WHERE THE MAIN BRITISH BATTERIES
WERE PLANTED.

ACROSS THE FORT AND DOWN THE VALLEY, FROM THE WEST ANGLE.

INTRODUCTORY.

THERE is no region throughout the country more replete with scenes of great historic interest (from the early date of the French and Indian wars to the war of 1812) than the Maumee Valley, and the most important and interesting of them come within the vision of one standing upon the breezy heights of old Ft. Meigs. The most prominent points, in chronological order, are the following :

1st. Ft. MIAMI, fifteen miles from the mouth of the river, on the north or left bank. Established in 1680, by an expedition sent there by Frontenac, Governor of Canada, it was a military and trading post and was soon abandoned. By order of Glencoe, the Canadian Governor, it was re-occupied in 1785 as a military post, and was so occupied when Gen. Anthony Wayne defeated the Indian nations, at the battle of "Fallen Timbers," August 20, 1794. In 1795 it was again abandoned, pursuant to treaty provisions between Great Britain and the United States. Again it was occupied by British soldiers under General Proctor during the siege of Ft. Meigs, in 1813. The outlines of some of its old bastions and embankments are still plain y defined.

2d. Ft. DEFIANCE. November 4, 1791, Gen. St. Clair, at the head of 2,000 regulars, had suffered a crushing defeat at the hands of the Indians at Greenville, Darke county, and soon afterward Gen. Anthony Wayne was placed in command of the Western army. Gen. Wayne built Ft. Greenville in December, 1793, and organized an army of 3,000 troops, among whom were 1,600 mounted Kentuckians under Gen. Scott. Late in July, 1794, with this army he commenced his march to the Miami of the Lakes (Maumee); August 8 they arrived at the confluence of the Miami of the Lakes and the Auglaize, where they found a highly cultivated country, with apple and peach orchards—evidences of the industry of the French and some of the most civilized Indian tribes. Here, with great rapidity and fine military engineering, a strong fort was built and appropriately named Ft. Defiance, the remains of which are still to be seen.

3d. FALLEN TIMBERS. August 16, 1794, Gen. Wayne, leaving a sufficient force at Ft. Defiance, moved down the left bank of the river; on the 18th a small fortification for the deposit of military stores was erected at Roch de Boeuf, a mile above the present village of Waterville, and named Ft. Deposit. Five miles below this point, on the morning of the 20th, Gen. Wayne's troops encountered the allied Indian forces commanded by the young and intrepid chief, Turkey Foot; the conflict, short, sharp and decisive, terminated in the overwhelming defeat of the Indians. It is known as the "Battle of Fallen Timbers," and was one of the most important in its results that had ever been fought with the Indian tribes, for it ended in a final treaty of peace at Greenville, and concluded the persecutions of the pioneer settlers. This was chosen by Turkey Foot as his battle-ground, because a hurricane had windrowed the forest trees, making an almost insurmountable obstruction to Wayne's mounted troops and a natural fortification for the Indians. Wayne, however, came upon them like the winds that had laid low the giants of the forest, his soldiers partaking of his own irresistible courage and fighting qualities; "Mad Anthony," by reason of this, was afterward known among the various Indian tribes as "Che-no-tin"—translated, "the Whirlwind." Near the base of Presque Isle Hill (an abrupt and narrow point of land, which extends like a promontory toward the river, and which was also a portion of the battle ground) and a few yards distant from the water, is an immense bowlder, afterward carved by the Indians with representations of turkeys' feet, in memory of their beloved chieftain who fell there during the conflict. Thus we are indebted to the savages for the only monument to mark the many historic spots in the valley. Lieut. Harrison (afterward Commander-in-Chief of the Northwestern army) was an aid-de-camp to Gen. Wayne in this campaign.

4th. FT. INDUSTRY. Wayne pursued the Indians down the river until they took refuge under the guns of Ft. Miami, then garrisoned by some British regulars under Major Campbell. The latter's warning to the American troops to keep their distance or he would fire upon them, was answered by a demand from Wayne to know the reason why British troops were thus occupying American territory ; the reply from Campbell was that he was acting under the orders of his superior officer, and that he should maintain his position unless otherwise instructed. Not feeling authorized, at this juncture, to open a war with Great Britain, Gen. Wayne marched his troops past the fort, out of range of the guns, and, halting at the mouth of Swan Creek, seven miles below, built Ft. Industry, and garrisoned it with a small force under Lieut. Rhea, by whom it continued to be occupied for several years. From this time until the raising of the second siege of Ft. Meigs, July 28, 1813, the British government held a precarious claim to the territory northwest of the Maumee river, and their agents from Canada influenced the Indians to aid them in holding it.

5th. FT. WAYNE. Upon the completion of Ft. Industry, Gen. Wayne marched his army back up the river to the present site of the city of Ft. Wayne, and there, in the fall of 1794, constructed the military fort which was named in his honor, at the confluence of the two rivers which form the Maumee; leaving it strongly garrisoned, he withdrew his main force to Greenville, where the famous treaty of peace was consummated with Little Turtle.

6th. FT. MEIGS. This, the most important and imposing of the fortifications in the Maumee Valley and the great Northwest, was constructed by Gen. Harrison's troops under the superintendence of Capt. Wood, of the engineer's corps, early in 1813, and is made the interesting subject of this sketch. The author has attempted the task with no pretensions of offering anything original, but, in view of the wide-spread interest which has recently been awakened in this historic spot, he gives to the public a compilation of facts and incidents taken from the best accredited authorities, including the official reports of General Harrison.

DOWN THE RAVINE TOWARD PERRYSBURG, FROM THE NORTH ANGLE, LOOKING
EAST; DUDLEY BURIAL GROUND ON THE RIGHT, MARKED BY A
DEAD WALNUT TREE.

HISTORICAL

DOWN THE SMALL RAVINE, OFF THE EAST ANGLE OF THE FORT.

IN April, 1812, the Indians, stimulated by the English in Canada, had become quite hostile along the waters of Lakes Erie, Huron and Michigan, and the inhabitants of the Michigan territory were utterly defenseless. War with England was imminent—a war to compel her to discontinue her violation of the treaty of 1783. A requisition was made by the President upon Gov. Meigs, of Ohio, for 1,200 militia to protect the border, and in obedience to the call, orders were issued to the Major-Generals of the western and middle divisions to furnish the r respective quotas of men, and rendezvous at Dayton, April 29. May 25 ollowing, Gen. Wm. Hull, having been appointed to conduct he expedition, took command, and the troops commenced the ine of march for the northwest July 1, proceeding via Staunton, Urbana, Ft. McArthur (on the Scioto), Ft. Necessity, Ft. Findlay on Blanchard's Fork of the Auglaize), thence to the foot of the apids of the Maumee river. From Ft. McArthur to the rapids he route was through a dense and trackless forest, 150 miles in ength. June 26, while at Ft. Findlay, Gen. Hull received dis-atches from the Secretary of War, notifying him that war had

been declared against England. Leaving Ft. Findlay June 27
the army arrived on the banks of the Maumee (near the site
afterward appropriated for the building of Ft. Meigs), on the
30th. One who was with Hull's army (writing the history of
the expedition in 1815), thus speaks of their arrival at the river
     "The 30th was a joyous day: the army suddenly emerged
from a gloomy wilderness, 150 miles in extent, to a full view of
the broad Miami (Maumee), and its elysian banks. Never was
the power of contrast more sensibly felt: in the rear stood a
boundless forest—the abode of frightful beasts of prey and unre
lenting savages; in front was presented to the ravished senses a
scene at once gay and magnificent beyond description. Under
the eyes rolled a beautiful river; on its opposite margin arose a
smiling village ; to the right and the left, as far as the eye could
reach, were seen enameled meadows clad in the rich luxuriance
of a summer's dress."
     At this point Lieut. Robt. Davidson, and twenty-five men of
Col. Cass' regiment, were left for the purpose of building a block
house, while the balance of the troops proceeded to Detroit, where
they arrived July 5; July 29, the British colonel, Proctor, placed
his troops at Malden, cutting off the supplies of the American
army from Ohio. August 16, Gen. Hull surrendered his whole
army. Mackinaw and Ft. Dearborn were soon afterward cap
tured by the Indians, and all of the northwest, excepting Ft
Wayne and Ft. Harrison (which were both attacked, the latter
being defended by troops under command of Zachary Taylor)
was in the hands of the British and Indians. At this time, at
the foot of the Maumee rapids was the only white settlement
between Lower Sandusky (Fremont) and Frenchtown (Monroe)
Mich.
     Previous to the surrender at Detroit, the Governors of Ohio
and Kentucky, in obedience to orders from the War Department
had sent powerful reinforcements to the aid of Gen. Hull, and
had he delayed the capitulation a few days, his army would have
been saved. The forces advancing to his support were 2,000
militia and Col. R. M. Johnston's battalion of mounted riflemen
of Kentucky, under Gen. Payne; a brigade of Ohio militia under
Gen. Tupper, of Gallia county, and 1,000 regulars under Gen
Winchester. They had arrived at the St. Marys river when the
news of the surrender reached them. It was a time when a

great military commander was needed to save the country from dire disaster. The Governor of Kentucky brevetted William Henry Harrison a Major-General, who was made Commander-in-Chief of the northwestern army, Sept. 17, 1812; it was while at Piqua that he first received the official dispatch from Washington notifying him of his appointment. His army then consisted of regular troops, rangers, volunteers and militia from Ohio and Kentucky, and detached militia and volunteers from Virginia and Pennsylvania. Major Stoddard, senior officer of artillery, was ordered to report to him with all of the artillery which could be collected; Major Denny, of Pittsburg, received the contract for furnishing supplies (stores and munitions), and Col. Buford, Deputy Commissioner, at Lexington, Ky., was supplied with funds subject to Gen. Harrison's order. Harrison's general instructions were to retake Detroit, with a view to the conquest of Upper Canada, and to penetrate that country as soo 1 as practicable. Gen. Harrison's plan was to collect the troops at Wooster, Urbana, Ft. Defiance and St. Marys, and from these points concentrate them at the foot of the rapids on the Maumee, the project of a forced march to Detroit being made an after consideration. The base line of the new campaign extended from Upper Sandusky to St. Marys, and these two places, with Ft. McArthur (near the present city of Kenton), were intended as the depots for provisions, artillery and military stores. The troops at Ft. Defiance were intended as a corps of observation, and were to advance to the foot of the rapids after the artillery had arrived at Upper Sandusky. A corps of observation was also stationed at Lower Sandusky (Fremont), the northeastern extremity of the military base. This arrangement covered the frontier at every threatened point, and the various quartermasters were busily engaged in accumulating supplies and transportation, n anticipation of the advance of the main army to the objective point—the foot of the rapids on the Maumee.

In the meantime, Gen. Winchester was in command of the troops at Ft. Wayne, still ignorant of the fact that Gen. Harrison had been appointed Commander-in-Chief. The latter was at St. Marys, where 3,000 troops had been collected, when information was received that a large force of British and Indians, with artillery, were passing up the left bank of the Maumee to attack Ft. Wayne, and feeling confident that Gen. Winchester's force was strong enough to resist the enemy, Gen. Harrison started with his troops on a forced march to Ft. Defiance to intercept them. This was early in October, 1812 ; the country was in a terrible condition, on account of recent heavy rains, and it was not until the close of the second day's weary march that the troops reached the Auglaize and encamped for the night. The march was resumed at daybreak the next morning, and in the course of the next day Gen. Harrison met an officer from Gen. Winchester, who informed him that the latter had advanced to Ft. Defiance, and the enemy had fled. Harrison arrived at Ft. Defiance that night. The day following he had a conference with Gen. Winchester, placing him in command of the left wing of the army, and assigning him his part in the contemplated general operations. Gen. E. W. Tupper (who had joined the army with about 1,000 volunteers, raised principally in his own county, Gallia, and Lawrence and Jackson counties), was given command of the central division, with headquarters at Ft. McArthur. Harrison took personal command of the right wing, with headquarters at Upper Sandusky.

At this time the main British troops, under Gen. Proctor, were at Detroit and Malden, and the officers were in ignorance of the military preparations in Ohio. Their Indian allies were raiding throughout the country, mostly in small detached bands, a large party of them being engaged in foraging for corn and hogs on the rich bottom lands along the Maumee rapids.

Several minor conflicts occurred with the Indians during the winter, but nothing of importance transpired until January 10, 1813, when Gen. Winchester arrived with his troops from Defiance at the foot of the rapids. Messengers reached him here from the inhabitants of Frenchtown (Monroe), on the river Raisin, imploring protection, as they were exposed to the hostility of the British and Indians. Thereupon, on January 17, Col. Lewis, with 550 men, was sent over the frozen waters of the river and lake to their succor, followed soon afterward with 110 more men under Col. Allen. They arrived on the afternoon of the 18th, and after a sharp conflict gained possession of the village, and immediately commenced the erection of defenses and sent for reinforcements. On the 19th Winchester started to support them with 259 men, reaching his destination the next evening. He committed the folly, however, of encamping on the open ground, neglecting the precaution of erecting earthworks or stationing advanced picket guards. At daybreak they were aroused by the discharge of grapeshot from a British battery, erected within 300 yards of their camp, and the yells of the savages who had surrounded them upon every side. The result was inevitable; and those of Winchester's troops who escaped death or capture (which were proportionately few in number), fled, Winchester and Lewis being among the prisoners. The party who were stationed behind their slight defenses still retained their position, but, under the order of Winchester (who was persuaded by Proctor's old argument of an irrepressible Indian massacre in case of continued resistance), they surrendered. The pernicious Proctor's pledge was broken, however, and the scene of massacre which followed on the succeeding night and day forms one of the most hideous chapters in the history of our country. Of the American army, over 900 strong, one-third were killed in battle, or in the massacre which followed, and but 33 escaped capture.

On the night of the 16th, Harrison (who was then at Upper Sandusky), received notice that Winchester with the left wing of the army had arrived at the foot of the Maumee rapids, and soon afterward of the expedition to the river Raisin; he at once proceeded to Lower Sandusky, and on the morning of the 18th sent forward a detachment of troops to the support of Winchester. On the 19th, Harrison started with additional troops, and on the morning of the 20th arrived at the Maumee rapids. The balance of Winchester's troops which he had left at the rapids (300 in number), and a regiment of Harrison's command, were also hastily dispatched to Frenchtown on the evening of the 21st and the morning of the following day. These troops, however, were met soon after they started by some of the survivors of the conflict, who told the terrible tale. It was decided by a council of officers that it would be needless and unwise to proceed farther, and the troops returned to the rapids. The next morning, in order to prevent the possibility of being cut off from their supplies, the troops retired to the Portage river, 18 miles back from Winchester's position, after first destroying the block-house that had been erected, together with such provisions as they could not carry away. Here Harrison awaited the arrival of expected reinforcements of troops and artillery, which were detained by the heavy rains and did not put in an appearance until January 30.

On February 1, with 1,700 men and a few pieces of artillery, Harrison again advanced to the foot of the rapids, where he took up a more commanding position than Winchester had selected. All troops were ordered to rendezvous at this point as quickly as possible, and the erection of Ft. Meigs was immediately commenced. Letters regarding the defeat of Winchester were received by Gov. Meigs from every part of the State, and the country was greatly alarmed.

THE PATRIOTIC RALLY TO HARRISON'S STANDARD, AS DESCRIBED BY A PARTICIPANT.

The following, from the pen of Rev. A. M. Lorraine, one of the Virginia troops at Ft. Meigs, will prove of interest in this connection :

"When the news of Hull's surrender reached the patriotic town of Petersburg, in Virginia, it overwhelmed the whole population with indignation and sorrow. Some of the most popular young men, with martial music and the American ensign, paraded the streets, and with impassioned appeals called on their youthful associates to march to the rescue. The scene that followed was soul-thrilling to the patriot. Clerks, mechanics and students of medicine and law rushed to the standard, and the placid farmer took the epidemic and fell in. In a few days a company of one hundred and four, richly uniformed, offered themselves to the government to serve twelve months under the banner of the brave Harrison, and no married man was admitted into the ranks.

"At an early hour in the day, the company marched to 'Center Hill,' which overlooked the town. There they were met by a delegation of ladies, who presented the company with a stand of colors, richly and tastily ornamented. Fond farewells were spoken, which, to many of the young men, were the last on earth to those they loved most dearly, and with knapsacks on our backs, we marched forth." *   *   *

The first night the company camped near Warebottom Church, and the next day they entered Richmond, escorted by a detachment of troops. Here another volunteer company was organized, and they started on the march for the Western frontier. On their route through Virginia they were feted and cheered in the most flattering manner. Passing by Monticello, they were given a grand reception by Thomas Jefferson. Climbing the Blue Ridge, they proceeded, via White Sulphur Springs, down the Great Kanawha, and crossing the Ohio river at Point Pleasant, soon reached Chillicothe, then the capital of Ohio. The legislature, which was then in session, gave them a grand feast, which was followed by one from the citizens. But now the Indian summer days had passed, and the trials and hardships of a soldier's life commenced. As they left Chillicothe, a bleak northwester began to blow, the rain and snow were driven in their faces, and the whole country became covered with the white mantle of winter. Through mud and ice and storms and swollen streams, they forced their way to Franklinton (a village on the Scioto, opposite the present city of Columbus), which was then the headquarters of the army. Lorraine continues:

"For the twelve succeeding months, our tender volunteers, most of whom had not passed their twentieth year, were exposed to labors, dangers, deprivation and death, of which their youthful minds had never conceived. We moved on through the plat of Columbus, where there was at that time only one house erected—albeit we left Franklinton in its meridian glory. Through most intolerable roads and severe weather, we reached the town of Delaware, then a handsome village—the *ultima thule* of American civilization, as far as our route was concerned. We passed only one cabin between this town and Upper Sandusky, and the plains of Crawford presented but a wild waste of crusted snow, through which we marched with excessive labor. When we reached the embodied host on the Sandusky river, our little band seemed to mingle as an atom in the long line which at daybreak was mustered on the high banks of the river."

At midnight, during a howling snow storm, the troops were aroused from slumber by a call to arms, and in a few minutes they were marching through the dark, dense forest, bound through the Black Swamp to reinforce Harrison, who, after Winchester's defeat, had fallen back on the Carrying (Portage) river. Led by a guide, the whole detachment followed in Indian file, laden with their accouterments. It was a tedious, trying, desperate march, which was alleviated somewhat after they struck Hull's road. The first day and night they marched thirty miles, and camped in the snow. After untold hardships they joined

Gen. Harrison's command on the banks of the Portage, and the whole army, without loss of time, moved on to the Maumee river four or five miles above Perrysburg (Winchester's old position) Here they encamped for the night, and the next morning (Feb 2, 1813), the whole command, with their heavy ordnance and baggage, marched down the frozen river in solid column to the foot of the rapids, where they halted on an elevated and commanding position.

BUILDING OF FT. MEIGS, FEBRUARY 2, 1813.

Here it was determined to take up winter quarters, and a hollow square was formed on the most commanding hill. Trees were felled and breastworks were thrown about the whole army before the troops were permitted to retire to rest. Their supper consisted of parched corn, which had been their only subsistence during the entire day ; the grain had been gathered from the rich bottom lands in their march down the river. For several subsequent weeks, the troops were employed daily in digging trenches, felling trees, splitting logs, setting up picketing (which was composed of the split logs), raising blockhouses, and doing everything necessary to fortify the post, which originally covered nine acres (afterward increased to about fourteen acres), and which, when finished, was named "Ft. Meigs," in honor of the patriotic governor of Ohio. Capt. Wood, of the engineer's corps, superintended the construction.

Mr. Lorraine states : "This season of fatigue was replete with hardships, as it was in the depth of winter, and we suffered from many privations. However, our bodies and minds were actively employed, which rendered our condition far preferable to what followed. The winter was unusually severe, and one unfortunate sentinel was found one morning at his post frozen to death."

DISPOSAL OF THE TROOPS AND PREPARATIONS FOR THE WINTER.

Gen. Harrison's design, when he rendezvoused his army at the foot of the Maumee rapids, was to make a vigorous attack upon the British and Indians at Malden, but he was prevented by circumstances over which he had no control. A January thaw had occurred which rendered roads almost impassable, and the trip over the ice utterly impossible. A number of wagons and sleds, loaded with ammunition and other munitions of war, were about twenty-four days making the trip from Upper Sandusky to the Maumee. The period of service of the Ohio and Kentucky troops who first took the field expired in February, but they expressed themselves perfectly willing to follow Harrison against the enemy without regard to the expiration of their term of enlistment—a term of fourteen months. In a dispatch to the Secretary of War, dated "Headquarters, foot of the Miami Rapids, Feb. 11, 1813," Gen. Harrison says:

"Having been joined by Gen. Leftraech, with his brigade, and a regiment of the Pennsylvania quota, at the Portage river, on the 30th ult., I marched from thence on the 1st inst., and reached this place on the morning of the 2d, with an effective force of sixteen hundred men. I have since been joined by a Kentucky regiment, and Gen. Tupper's Ohio brigade, which has increased our numbers to two thousand non-commissioned officers and privates. * * * I have ordered the whole of the troops of the left wing (excepting one company for each of the six forts in that quarter), the balance of the Pennsylvania brigade, and the Ohio brigade under Gen. Tupper, and a detachment of regular troops of twelve-months' volunteers under command of Col. Campbell, to march to this place as soon as possible. * * * The disposition of the troops for the remainder of the winter will be as follows: A battalion of militia lately called out from this State, with the company of troops now at Ft. Winchester [Defiance.] will garrison the posts upon the waters of the Auglaize and St. Marys. The small blockhouses upon Hull's trace, will have a subaltern's command in each. A company will be placed at Upper Sandusky, and another at Lower Sandusky. All the rest of the troops will be brought to this place, amounting to from 1,500 to 1,800 men. I am erecting here a pretty strong fort—capable of resisting field artillery at least. The troops will be placed in a fortified camp, covered on one flank by the fort. This is the best position that can be taken to cover the frontier, and the small posts in the rear of it, and those above it on the Miami [Maumee] and its waters. The force placed here ought, however, to be strong enough to encounter any that the enemy may detach against the forts above. Twenty-five hundred would not be too many. But, anxious to reduce the expenses during the winter within as narrow bounds as possible, I have desired the Governor of Kentucky not to call out (but to hold in readiness to march) the 1,500 men lately required of him. All the teams which have been hired for the public service will be discharged, and those belonging to the public, which are principally oxen, disposed of in the settlements, where forage is cheaper, and every other arrangement made which will lessen the expenses during the winter. Attention will still, however, be paid to the deposit of supplies for the ensuing campaign. Immense supplies of provisions have been accumulating upon the Auglaize river, and boats and pirogues prepared to bring them down as soon as the river opens."

A BOLD BUT UNSUCCESSFUL ENTERPRISE.

On Friday, February 26, a company of men, who had volunteered their services to go upon a bold and desperate enterprise, was sent out by Gen. Harrison from the fort, with instructions to rendezvous at a blockhouse located upon the site subsequently occupied by Ft. Stephenson, at Lower Sandusky, which was at that time the northern outpost of the military base, and garrisoned by two companies of militia. The force, which was under the command of Capt. Langham, consisted of 220 regulars and Virginia and Pennsylvania militia, and 22 Indians; total, 242, besides guides and sled drivers.

March 2, they left the Lower Sandusky blockhouse, with six days' provisions, and after proceeding about a mile down the Portage river, they were halted and informed by Capt. Langham that the object of the expedition was to cross over the frozen lake to Malden, and, in the darkness of the night, destroy, with combustibles, the British fleet and the military stores upon the river's bank; then retreat in their sleighs to a point on Maumee Bay, where they were to be met by a large force under Harrison, who would cover their retreat to the fort. The proximity of Indian and French spies rendered the enterprise exceedingly hazardous, and an opportunity was given to those who desired to withdraw. About twenty militiamen and a half-dozen Indians took advantage of this liberty, and the balance continued on down the river in sleighs, across Sandusky Bay and the peninsula at the left, to the lake shore, where they encamped for the night; being without tents they became thoroughly wet from the snow and rain, and thirteen of the militia, and several of the Indians, with a chief, turned back. In the morning they crossed the ice, a distance of seventeen miles, to Middle Bass Island. In the afternoon they discovered sled tracks in the snow, leading from the direction of Sandusky Bay toward Malden, and it was rightly conjectured that they had been made by a couple of French spies, who had gone to inform the enemy. At the north of the island, the ice was discovered to be weak and broken up in the distance; the weather continued to be very mild, and as the guides declared that a continuation of the trip was impracticable and sure to prove disastrous, they returned by way of Presque Isle, at which point they met Gen. Harrison with a body of troops, and from thence they proceeded to Ft. Meigs in safety. On their return journey they found the lake open near West Sister Island. No doubt the expedition would have been a grand success if it could have been made earlier in the season.

ADVENTURES WITH THE INDIANS.

On March 9, the day being fine, several of the soldiers started from the fort, and crossing the river went down as far as Ft. Miami on a hunting expedition. They were discovered by a roving band of Indians, who fired upon them and then fled. One man received a leaden ball in the leaves of a Bible, which he carried in his breast pocket. Lieut. Walker was killed; his remains were recovered the next day, and buried on the parade ground of the fort, where they still lie. The others arrived at the fort unharmed.

Early in April, a small body of Canadian French volunteers, who had enlisted under Harrison, were reconnoitering in a boat along the narrow channel north of the large island just above Ft. Miami, when they were attacked by a band of Indians who had suddenly advanced to meet them in two large canoes which had been concealed on the shore. A desperate hand-to-hand conflict ensued, during which all of the whites but the commanding officer and two of his men were either killed or wounded, and all of the savages but one were slain. As the whites were returning to the fort they saw this solitary brave sit up in one of the canoes and paddle feebly to the shore.

OPENING OF THE SIEGE OF FT. MEIGS.

Late in March, Gen. Harrison, anticipating the advance of the British from Malden as soon as the ice broke up, went to the interior to bring forward some of the reserve troops, and despatched Capt. Wm. Oliver with an order for the Kentucky troops to hasten forward. April 12th he returned with a detachment of troops and applied himself earnestly to the strengthening of Ft. Meigs, recognizing the fact that it must stand as the grand bulwark of defense for the thousands of square miles of territory lying between the Ohio river and the great lakes.

On the breaking up of the ice in Lake Erie, Gen. Proctor, with all his available forces, moved up the left bank of the Maumee for the purpose of laying siege to Ft. Meigs. According to British reports, this force consisted of 500 regulars and Canadian militia from Malden and 1,500 Indians under Tecumseh (a total of 2,000, afterward increased about one-half), accompanied by a train of battering artillery, attended by two gunboats; one of the battering guns was a twenty-four pounder. The main British camp was established at Ft. Miami. One of the Virginia Volunteers at Ft. Meigs, in speaking of this exciting period, says:

" On the afternoon of April 26, as numbers were gathered together on the parade, two strangers, finely mounted, appeared on the opposite bank of the river, and seemed to be taking a very calm and deliberate survey of our works. The circumstance was a suspicious one, and in order to ascertain their business a messenger was sent across the river in the shape of a ball from one of our heavy guns, which tore up the earth about them and put them to a hasty flight. If that ball had struck its mark, much bloodshed might have been prevented, for we subsequently learned that our illustrious visitors were Proctor and Tecumseh. The garrison was immediately employed in building immense traverses across the fort, taking down the tents and preparing for a siege. The work accomplished in a few hours, under the excitement of the occasion, was prodigious. The grand traverse being completed, each mess was ordered to excavate, under the embankment, suitable lodgings as substitutes for tents. Those rooms were shot-proof and bomb-proof, except in the event of a shell falling in the traverse and at the mouth of a cave." These bomb-proofs were drained by a ditch cut through the heavy outside embankment to the slope of the hill, and some of them had floors laid with brick, flat stones and timber. The well which had been commenced inside the fort was not yet completed, and many men were afterward shot while engaged in the perilous task of supplying the garrison with water from the river. During the strengthening of the works, Gen. Harrison was present everywhere, encouraging his men in their labors.

April 27 the enemy established three gun batteries and one mortar battery on the left bank of the river, directly opposite the fort; the present sites of the Methodist and Presbyterian churches in Maumee, and a point midway between them, indicate, as nearly as can be ascertained, the location of the gun batteries, and on the prominent point on the river's bank, in the lower part of town, the mortar battery was planted; all were well protected by earthworks, which at the latter point are still well preserved. For some distance around the fort, on every side, the timber had all been cut and used in the construction of the stockade and blockhouses; this open space gave free play to the artillery and small arms and prevented a surprise from the Indians. On the evening of the 27th, the main body of Indians was conveyed across the river in boats and they surrounded the garrison. On the 29th, the siege began in earnest, all communication being cut off, and firing from that time continued briskly on both sides. Gen. Harrison gave his personal attention to every detail, seeming to be perfectly indifferent to the danger to which he exposed himself, and he met with many narrow escapes. According to his orders, one-third of the men were continually on active duty. Many of these young heroes here had their first taste of battle, and they afterward received the deserved congratulations of their beloved commander for their brave gallantry and unshrinking devotion. A. M. Lorraine, in telling his interesting story of the siege, says:

"One of our militia men took his station on the embankment and gratuitously forewarned us of every shot. In this he became so skillful that he could, in almost every case, predict the destination of the ball. As soon as he saw the smoke issue from the muzzle of the gun, he would cry out 'shot' or 'bomb' as the case might be — 'Look out, main battery' — 'Blockhouse No 1' — 'Now for the meat house' — 'Good-bye if you will pass.' The brave fellow continued to maintain his post, despite the expostulations of his friends, until one shot came which defied all his calculations. Silent, motionless, perplexed, he stood for a moment, and then he was swept into eternity. In his zeal, the unfortunate hero forgot to consider that when there was no obliquity in the issue of the smoke, either to the right or left above or below, the fatal messenger was traveling in the direct line of his vision. On the most active day of the investment, as many as five hundred shots and bombs were hurled at our fort. Meantime, the Indians, from their positions in the branches of the nearest trees, fired incessantly at us over the stockade, but they were so distant that little serious execution was done, many of the balls falling to the ground before they reached their destination. The number killed in the fort was small considering the profuse expenditure of ball and powder. Many of the wounded had to suffer the amputation of limbs.

"The most dangerous duty which we performed within the precincts of the fort was in covering the magazine. Previous to this the powder had been deposited in wagons and these stationed in the grand traverse. Here there was no security against bombs and it was therefore thought prudent to remove the powder into a small blockhouse and cover it with earth. The enemy, judging our design from our movements, now directed all their shot at this point, and many of their balls were red-hot. Whereve they struck they produced a cloud of smoke and made a frightful hissing. An officer, passing our quarters, said, 'Boys, who will volunteer to cover the magazine?' Fired with patriotic zeal away several of us went, and as we reached the spot a ball from the enemy's guns took off the head of one of our party. How the dirt flew from the shovels in our nervous hands! While we were desperately at work a bomb shell fell upon the roof, and lodging in one of the braces, commenced spinning. Instantly we fell prostrate on our faces, and, in breathless horror, awaited the tremendous explosion which we expected to end our earthly career. Only one of the party exercised his calm reason, and silently argued that, as the shell had not exploded as quickly as usual, something might be wrong in its arrangement. In an event, death was inevitable if it was not extinguished, and the brave fellow, springing to his feet, seized a boat hook, pulled the hissing bomb to the ground and jerked the burning fuse from its socket. It was then discovered that the shell was filled with inflammable matter, which, if once exploded, would have spread flames on all around. Immediately resuming our labors, we were soon relieved by the welcome intelligence that the magazine was safe, and we could go to our lines."

On the night of April 30, the enemy towed a gunboat up near the fort and fired point blank shot for some time, without effect, and they retired from their position as soon as it was light enough for them to be seen by the gunners at the fort. May 1, the enemy fired 256 times from their gun batteries, and their 24-pound shot passed through the pickets without displacing them; eight Americans were wounded that day, and a bullet struck the seat on which Harrison was sitting. May 2, the enemy fired 457 cannon shot; the American loss was one killed and ten wounded: several were slightly injured by the Indian bullets fired from the trees. May 3, the fierce firing of bombs and cannon balls continued, at intervals, all day; an Indian, from a tree, shot one man through the head, and he was in turn brought down by a Kentucky sharpshooter; six others were killed by bombs and solid shot; the enemy fired 516 shots during the day, and 47 at night.

On the night of May 3, a gun and mortar battery, with about 200 regulars were transported on the gunboats across the river from the British camp at Ft. Miami, and secretly fortified themselves in an arm of the broad ravine which extends in a northeast direction from the fort. This position was about 400 yards distant from the fort, and the earthworks which were erected are still to be seen near the southwest boundary of Ft. Meigs cemetery. The morning of the 4th opened with rain, which retarded the fire of the enemy. The erection of the battery in the ravine was soon discovered at the fort, and short traverses were quickly thrown up at right angles with the grand traverse, to protect the troops from their fire. At this time, Harrison received a summons from Proctor to surrender, the messenger (Major Chambers) bombastically exaggerating the means at his command. Gen. Harrison's historic reply was: "Assure the general that he will never have this post surrendered to him upon any terms. Should it fall into his hands, it will be in a manner calculated to do him more honor, and to give him larger claims upon the gratitude of his government, than any capitulation could possibly do."

ARRIVAL OF REINFORCEMENTS UNDER GEN. CLAY.

At about 12 o'clock on the night of May 4, Capt. William Oliver, skillfully avoiding the Indians, found his way into the fort after a perilous journey, with a welcome message from Gen. Green Clay, stating that he was on his way down the river with 1,200 Kentuckians in flat boats; he could reach the fort in two hours, and had halted to await orders. Harrison immediately dispatched Capt. Hamilton with orders for Gen. Clay to detach 800 men from his brigade, who were directed to land on the left bank of the river, one and one half miles above the fort, "march from thence to the British batteries, take possession of their cannon, spike them, cut down their carriages, return to their boats and cross over to the American fort." The remainder of Clay's force were ordered to land on the right bank and fight their way to the fort, while sorties were to be made from the garrison to aid them. Capt. Hamilton proceeded up the river in a pirogue and stationed a man on the right bank, one and one half miles above the fort, to act as a pilot to conduct Gen. Clay, with the last mentioned detachment, into the entrenchments; he then crossed over and stationed his pirogue at the place designated for the other division to land.

Having received his instructions, Gen. Clay moved forward en masse, each officer taking his position according to rank. Col. Dudley, being senior in command, led the van, and, with the troops occupying the first twelve boats, landed at the place designated without difficulty. Gen. Clay, with the remainder of his troops (400), commenced disembarking on the right bank opposite Dudley's landing, but not finding the guide mentioned to him by Capt. Hamilton, he attempted to cross over to join Dudley; this being prevented by the swift current, he again attempted to land upon the right bank, and succeeded in doing so with only fifty of his men, amid a brisk fire from the enemy on shore, and made his way to the fort. The other boats, under command of Col. Boswell, were driven farther down the current, and landed on the left bank to join Dudley; they were ordered back however, and recrossed the river to make another attempt to reach the fort; after landing, the Indians attacked them but retreated, and the troops followed them up, leaving their boats, containing their baggage and a few sick, unprotected; a party of savages made a detour, and these sick men were tomahawked and the baggage plundered; a detachment of troops under Major Ball came to the rescue, and Boswell's command reached the fort with small loss.

MASSACRE OF COL. DUDLEY'S TROOPS.

In the meantime. Col. Dudley's command of nearly eight hundred men, carried out the perilous and important duty assigned them, but with most disastrous results to themselves. The following thrilling particulars of the affair are compiled from the account given by Lieut. Joseph R. Underwood, one of the participants attached to a company of Kentucky volunteers under Capt. John C. Morrison's command :

"The whole number of troops that landed amounted probably to 700 men. We were formed on the shore in three parallel lines, and ordered to march for the battery at right angles with the river. So far as I understand the plan of attack, one line was to form the line of battle in the rear of the battery parallel with the river; the other two lines to form one above and one below the battery, at right angles to the river. The lines thus formed advanced as silently as possible, the object being to surprise the enemy. Before we reached the battery, however, we were discovered by some straggling Indians, who fired upon us and then retreated. Our men, pleased at seeing them run, and perceiving that we were discovered, no longer deemed silence necessary, and raised a tremendous shout. This was the first intimation that the enemy received of our approach, and it so alarmed them that they abandoned the battery without any resistance, and the guns were successfully spiked. Capt. Morrison's company was formed on the river's bank above the battery. While passing through a hazel thicket toward the river, I saw Col. Dudley for the last time; he railed at me for not keeping my men in better line; I replied that it was impossible, owing to the condition of the ground and the obstacles in the way. We halted near the river bank; some of the enemy had got into our rear and were firing into us, and our company hastened to join the combatants at our front; falling in at the left of the regiment, we were soon in the midst of the conflict. The Indians attempted to flank us, and we drove them over a mile back from the river; from behind trees and logs, they poured a most destructive fire into us, and we charged upon them from time to time. Capt. Morrison fell, shot through the temples, the ball cutting the optic nerve and depriving him of sight. After caring for him as well as circumstances would allow, I assumed command of the company.

"At length we were ordered to fall back, keeping up a retreating fire, and as soon as this was done, the Indians advanced with savage yells. A temporary halt was twice made, but our ranks were soon in confusion, and a general rout occurred; the retreating army gathered about the battery and attempted to repel the onslaught. About this time, I received a ball in my back and was made prisoner, and informed that the whole army had surrendered.

"On our way to the garrison, we were stripped of the principal part of our clothing and valuables. As we neared the garrison at Ft. Miami, the Indians formed a line to the left of the road, there being a perpendicular bank on the right, near where the road passed. Here we were obliged to run the gauntlet into the fort, the Indians whipping, shooting and tomahawking their prisoners as they passed. By running as closely as possible to the muzzles of their guns, I escaped with the exception of some severe strokes over the back with their ramrods. Nearly forty Americans were killed in passing the line of savages. As I entered the ditch surrounding the garrison, the man in front of me was shot and I fell over his dead body; those following stumbled over us, and the passageway was thus blocked for a few moments. After entering the fort, the horrible tragedy was continued. A painted Indian mounted the dilapidated wall and shot one of the prisoners nearest him, and deliberately loading, shot again, the second ball giving two men a death wound; he then laid down his gun, and drawing his tomahawk, leaped among the defenseless prisoners and killed two others. The horror of the moment is indescribable; the excitement among the Indians was increasing, and a wholesale massacre seemed inevitable, as the weak protest of the British officers who were present, was entirely unavailing."

A British account of this terrible occurrence says: "The frenzy of these wretches knew no bounds, and an old veteran of the 41st was shot through the heart while endeavoring to wrest a victim from the grasp of his murderer; in all, forty of the unhappy prisoners were killed by the savages."

The manner in which a sudden end was put to the tragic scene is thus graphically described by William G. Ewing, in a letter to John H. James, Esq., of Urbana: "While this bloodthirsty carnage was raging, a thundering voice was heard in the rear, in the Indian tongue, and Tecumseh [on his return from the battle in the ravine across the river] was seen coming with all the rapidity his horse could carry him. Drawing near to where two Indians were in the act of killing one of the prisoners, he sprang from his horse, caught one by the throat and the other by the breast and threw them to the ground; drawing his tomahawk and scalping knife, he ran in between the Americans and Indians, brandishing them with the fury of a madman, and daring any of the hundreds who surrounded him to attempt to murder another prisoner. They all appeared confused and immediately desisted. His mind appeared rent with passion, and he exclaimed, almost with tears in his eyes, 'Oh, what will become of my Indians!' He then demanded, in an authoritative tone, where Proctor was, and nervously casting his eyes about and seeing that officer at a short distance, he sternly inquired why he had not put a stop to the inhuman massacre. 'Sir,' said Proctor, 'your Indians cannot be commanded.' 'Begone!' retorted Tecumseh, in the greatest disdain; 'you are unfit to command; go and put on petticoats.'"

Late in the afternoon the prisoners were placed in open boats and conveyed to the British ships, nine miles down the river. At the end of six days they were all discharged on parole. The expedition had been a success, as far as spiking the British guns was concerned, but the impetuous gallantry of these brave Kentuckians had rendered it a dearly bought one, as only about 150 of the 800 escaped; the balance were either killed or captured, Col. Dudley being among the slain.

After Dudley had spiked the batteries, some of his men loitered on the bank and filled the air with cheers. Harrison and a group of officers who were anxiously watching them from the main battery, with a presentiment of the sad fate which awaited them, earnestly beckoned them to return, but supposing that they

were returning their cheers, they reiterated their shouts o
triumph. Harrison, seeing this, exclaimed, in tones of anguish
"They are lost! Can I never teach my men the necessity of a
strict obedience to orders?" He then offered a thousand dollar
reward to any man who would cross the river and apprise then
of their danger. This was undertaken by an officer, but upon hi
arrival on the shore, and before he could launch his pirogue and
reach the middle of the river, the enemy had appeared in force
from below.

CAPTURE OF THE BRITISH BATTERY NEAR THE FORT.

Just prior to the time that these tragic events were occurring
on the left bank of the river, one more successful was transpiring
on the opposite side, near the fort. A detachment of troop
under Col. John Miller, of the 19th U. S. regiment, consisting o
about 250 of the 17th and 19th regiments, 100 volunteers and
Capt. Sebree's company of Kentucky militia (total 850 men
left the fort for the purpose of capturing the British two-gun
battery that had been stationed about 400 yards from the for
on the night of the 3d. The troops were drawn up in the smal
ravine under the southeast curtain of the fort, out of sight of th
enemy and out of reach of their fire ; to reach the battery, afte
passing out from this ravine, it was necessary to ascend the hil
to the right, in full view of the enemy, and pass over a plain o
two hundred yards in width into the woods, whence they pur
posed making a slight detour and come onto the enemy by a
flank movement. The battery was protected by 200 Britisl
regulars, two companies of Canadian militia and a large body o
Indians under Tecumseh. After passing along the ranks, en
couraging his men, Gen. Harrison took a position upon th
battery at the rear right angle to witness the contest. Th
troops advanced with their loaded arms trailed, and as the
reached the summit of the hill, they received the fire of th
British infantry, which did little harm ; the Indians fired fror
the woods with more deliberate aim, however, and did greate
execution. After the American troops had advanced about fift
yards onto the plain, they halted, closed their ranks and made
determined charge, firing as they advanced. Many of the enem
were killed and the balance fled. Gen. Harrison, who had bee
anxiously watching the result, at this juncture dispatched Majo

Todd with fifty regulars in pursuit of the foe, and they soon returned with two officers and forty-three non-commissioned officers and privates as prisoners.

RAISING OF THE SIEGE—BURIAL OF THE DEAD — COMPLIMENTS FROM GEN. HARRISON.

From the 6th to the 9th there was no firing. Flags of truce passed between the two armies, and an exchange of prisoners took place. On the morning of the 9th (the fourteenth day after the commencement of hostilities) as his Indian allies were threatening to desert him, Proctor raised the siege and retreated with his troops in all possible haste to Amherstburg. After their departure, a detachment was sent out to scour the woods and gather up the dead. The bodies, all more or less mutilated, were brought in great numbers to the fort and laid out before one of the gates. The next day they were committed to earth with military honors; all the cannon were fired in slow succession, and their deep reverberations rolled echoing in solemn cadence along the valley. The bodies of about forty-five heroes of Dudley's command were recovered and buried on the brow of the hill, about fifty yards northeast of the east angle of the fort. Their graves still remain undisturbed, covered with green sod, and a dead walnut tree is the only monument which marks the sacred spot.

The most authentic accounts attainable estimate the British force under Proctor, during the siege, at 2,560 men consisting of 560 regulars, 800 Canada militia, and 1,200 Indians. Harrison's force (including the troops which reached the fort on the morning of the 5th under Gen. Clay), was 2,000, about 100 of whom were unfit for duty at the opening of the siege. In his official report, Gen. Harrison states that the Indians were the most efficient force of the enemy. In this report he compliments his whole command for their efficiency, and especially mentions the following, on account of their meritorious service: Capt. Wood, commanding the corps of engineers, who superintended the construction of the fortifications; Maj. Stoddard, Capt. Gratiot, and Capt. Cushing, of the artillery; Capt. Hall, Col. Miller, Maj. Todd, Maj. Sodwick, Maj. Ritzer, Maj. Johnson, Adjt. Brown, Privates Peters, Lion and Timberlee, Sergts. Henderson, Tommes and Meldrum; Brig.-Gen. Clay, Col. Boswell, Maj. Fleacher; Capts.

Dudley, Simons, Medcalf and Sebree; the Pittsburg Blues, led by Lieut. McGee; the Petersburg volunteers and Lieut. Drum's detachment: the detachments of the 17th and 19th U. S. regiments, under Capts. Croghan, Bradford, Langham, Elliott and Nering; Lieuts. Campbell, Gwynn, Lee, Kercheval and Rees; Ensigns Shep, Hawkins, Harrison, Mitchell and Stockton; the members of his staff: Maj. Hukill, acting Inspector General, Majs. Graham and J. Johnson, Lieut. O'Fallon and deputy quartermaster Eubank. The General adds, referring to Dudley's command: "It rarely occurs that a general has to complain of the excessive ardor of his men, yet such appears always to be the case whenever the Kentucky militia are engaged; it is, indeed, the source of all their misfortunes; Dudley unsuccessfully attempted to restrain their rash ardor; such temerity is scarcely less fatal, although not so disgraceful, as cowardice."

Among those, also, who performed distinguished services under Harrison, were Peter Navarre and his brothers, Capt. Wm. Oliver, Capt. Leslie Coombs, Capt. McCune and James Doolan, who were employed as scouts. Peter Navarre was born in Detroit in 1796, and lived near the shore of Maumee Bay until his death.

The official returns of the killed and wounded at the siege of Ft. Meigs, and the several sorties of May 5 (not including those killed under Dudley), are as follows: Killed, 81; wounded, 189; total, 270; of these, 17 were killed and 65 wounded within the fortification.

Among the killed, not heretofore mentioned, was Lieut. McCullough, who was shot while conversing with General Harrison. His remains lie buried beside those of Lieut. Walker, on the parade ground of the fort.

THE SECOND SIEGE OF FT. MEIGS.

After the raising of the siege at Ft. Meigs, Gen. Harrison repaired the damage occasioned by the enemy's guns, and materially strengthened his position. Upon his recommendation the plan of the campaign had been changed; vessels were being built at Erie and Cleveland, and until these were ready it was determined to act upon the defensive. May 12th he departed for the interior to push the recruiting service and prepare for the approaching campaign, leaving Gen. Green Clay in command of the fort. July 20, the enemy was discovered ascending the river, and a party of ten men were surprised by the Indians, only three escaping death or capture. The number of troops with which Gen. Proctor had returned to subjugate the little garrison at Ft. Meigs was estimated at 5,000, including the largest band of Indians under Tecumseh that had ever assembled together during the war.

The night of their arrival, Gen. Clay dispatched Capt. McCune, of the Ohio militia, to Gen. Harrison, at Lower Sandusky, to notify him of the presence of the enemy. After delivering his message, Capt. McCune was ordered to return to the fort and instruct Gen. Clay to guard carefully against surprise, and he would have reinforcements there as soon as possible. Gen. Harrison also sent an order to Gen. McArthur to come with as many troops as he could muster, saying that the force at Ft. Meigs was too weak for anything but defensive operations, unless promptly reinforced.

Capt. McCune was sent out the second time with information to Gen. Harrison that a body of Indians were passing up the Maumee to attack Ft. Winchester (Defiance). The General, however, believed this movement of the enemy to be a ruse to cover their designs upon Upper and Lower Sandusky and Cleveland, and, after sending out a reconnoitering party to watch, he sent Capt. McCune back to the fort to report. The latter was accompanied on his return by James Doolan, a celebrated French Canadian scout; on arriving near the fort, about daybreak, they encountered the Indians and met with some exciting adventures and hair-breadth escapes before finally arriving safely within the enclosure; by listening they had obtained some valuable information regarding Tecumseh's plans, which proved of great value to the garrison.

On the evening of July 26, the British infantry secreted themselves in the ravine below the fort, the cavalry were in the adjacent woods, and the Indians were stationed in the forest near the Lower Sandusky road, about half a mile southeast from the fort. About dark they commenced a sham battle among themselves to deceive the Americans into the belief that a desperate conflict was transpiring between them and the expected reinforcements, in the hopes of enticing the garrison to the aid of their comrades; if the ruse proved successful, the British infantry and cavalry were to make a dash from their concealment on the left, thus cutting them off from retreat and capturing the fort. It was a cunning stratagem, and, had it not been met with equal cunning, the result of the war in the Northwest would probably have been different.

At the first sound of the supposed conflict, the garrison flew to arms; Gen. Clay ordered them to keep a keen watch, awaiting developments, but not to leave the fort. As the roar of musketry, mingled with the piercing savage yells increased, the troops insisted on being allowed to hasten to the rescue; it seemed to them that the lives of their beloved commander Harrison and their brave comrades were being sacrificed, while they stood idly by without raising a helping hand. It was a trying moment; Gen. Clay's explanation of the affair did not half satisfy them; some of the officers sided in opinion with the troops, and it was only their confidence in the courage and good judgment of Gen. Clay that prevented open insubordination and their destruction.

After keeping up a brisk firing and yelling for about half an hour, a shower of rain commenced falling and the firing gradually ceased. Before this, however, from the fact that no American troops could be seen endeavoring to reach the fort, the garrison were fully convinced of the deception. Finding their cunning ruse a failure, and fearing the arrival of large reinforcements, the enemy remained about the fort but one day longer, and on July 28 embarked, with their stores, down the lake. Thus closed the second siege of Ft. Meigs, triumphantly to the American arms.

IMPORTANT EVENTS SUBSEQUENT TO THE SIEGE OF FT. MEIGS.

Having raised the siege of Ft. Meigs, the British sailed around into Sandusky bay, while a large force of their Indian allies marched overland to co operate with them in an attack on Lower Sandusky, anticipating that the attention of the American troops would be directed toward Ft. Meigs and Defiance. Harrison had taken the precaution, however, of keeping patrols down the bay near the mouth of the Portage, who informed him of the enemy's arrival. On the 29th he received intelligence from Gen. Clay of what had transpired, and immediately called a council of war with McArthur, Cass, Ball, Paul, Wood, Hukill, Holmes and Graham, who decided that, as Ft. Stephenson at Lower Sandusky was a comparatively unimportant point, and that the defenses were too small to accommodate a garrison of over 200 troops, they would not reinforce the place, but destroy it and withdraw Major Croghan and his little band who were stationed there. An order to this effect was sent to the latter; before it reached him, however, the country was infested with the savages, and the determination was made to hold the fort or die. The British troops were landed soon afterward; a demand to surrender was refused and the subsequent successful defense of Ft. Stephenson was one of the most gallant and heroic in the history of the nation. Speaking of Maj. Croghan, in his official report of the affair, Gen. Harrison said: "It will not be among the least of Gen. Proctor's mortifications, that he has been baffled by a youth who has just passed his twenty-first year. He is a hero worthy of his gallant uncle, Gen. Geo. R. Clarke." Maj. Croghan was brevetted Lieutenant-Colonel by the President for his gallantry.

The defense of Ft. Stephenson, which occurred Aug. 2, 1813, was followed, on Sept. 10, by Commodore Perry's victory at Put-n-Bay—one of the most brilliant naval affairs in the history of any nation.

This victory removed the principal barrier to the commencement of active operations toward the recovery of the Michigan territory, and immediate steps were taken for an advance to Malden, and the troops (nearly 7,000) rendezvoused at the mouth of the Portage. Sept. 17, Gov. Shelby arrived there with 4,000 Kentuckians; Gen. Cass, with his brigade, came to Upper Sandusky; Col. Hill came with a regiment of Pennsylvania volunteers from Erie; on Sept. 20, Gen. McArthur came with his brigade from Ft. Meigs, leaving Col. Johnson's mounted regiment here as a garrison, with orders to subsequently march to Detroit by land. The troops were conveyed to Put-in-Bay in boats; on Sept. 25 they re-embarked for the Canadian shore, and on the 27th entered Malden, without encountering either British troops or Indians, who had retreated; the enemy continued their retreat from before Detroit, and on the 29th, the victorious Americans marched into that town; on the 30th, Col. Johnson's mounted rifle regiment arrived from Ft. Meigs. Oct. 2, the Americans commenced their pursuit of Proctor, whom they overtook and defeated in the battle of the Thames, Oct. 5, which practically closed the war in the northwest.

MAUMEE RIVER.

BOTTOM LAND.

WELL

TRAVERSE

GRAND

N

P

T

S

DESCRIPTIVE.

FT. MEIGS occupies a level plateau, located on the southeast bank of the Maumee, sixty feet above the water, about one-half mile above Perrysburg. Standing on its breezy height, the vision extends for a range of over twenty miles up and down the valley. The location was no doubt originally selected as a site for the fort on account of its expansive outlook, as well as its strong natural defenses, for certainly there is no spot in the State, or in the territory for many miles west and northwest, that will favorably compare with it as a point of extensive observation and scenic beauty. From above for many miles the silvery waters are seen, sparkling and flashing in their rapid flow over their rocky bed, winding among the pretty green islands and past the rich bottom lands, covered with ripening grain.

At the foot of the fort the rapids end, and the head of steam navigation commences. The river continues its winding way among the islands and bottom lands, but widens perceptibly after leaving the fort. The banks are lined with groups of native forest trees, thrifty orchards and vineyards and pretty residences. Ten miles below, over a low-lying headland, the church spires and many of the lofty buildings in the growing city of Toledo, come into view.

As one stands upon the old fort and drinks in this beautiful vision, he is overcome with sympathizing pity for the savage natives who named the river the "Mother of Waters," and to whom it was so fondly endeared that many brave lives were sacrificed in struggling to retain it from the grasp of the white man.

The outlook from Ft. Meigs embraces many miles in extent, and every foot of the soil within range of the vision has been made sacred by deeds of heroism in the history of the country. A broad ravine, leading from the fort on the right, affords a glimpse of the pretty town of Perrysburg, half hidden by the luxuriant trees which line its broad avenues, and on the brow of a small arm of the ravine are still to be seen the outlines of a British battery which did terrible execution during the siege, and was gallantly captured. In the foreground, a few rods from the fort, on a green hill-top, is the burial spot of forty-five of Dudley's brave command, whose graves have never been disturbed. To the left of this ravine, leading toward the river, twenty rods from the fort, is an elevated, narrow point known as "Indian Hill," where Gen. Harrison located an advance picket guard ; it was the site of an extensive Indian cemetery, which fact gave it its name.

One mile down the river on the opposite side, is the village of Miami—the site of Ft. Miami, occupied by the British General Proctor during the siege. Across the river, opposite Ft. Meigs, is the town of Maumee, famous in historic lore ; occupying a prominent position on a bluff bank, in the lower part of town, were located the British mortar batteries during the unpleasantness, and the outlines are still distinctly visible ; on the site of the Presbyterian and M. E. Churches were planted the main British gun batteries which did such terrible execution, and were captured by Col. Dudley's gallant command. About two miles above Maumee is Presque Isle Hill, the scene of the "Battle of Fallen Timbers."

PRESENT APPEARANCE OF FT. MEIGS.

Many of the heroes who defended Ft. Meigs in 1813, have visited the spot in late years, and have expressed their surprise that the original contour of the fort has been so well preserved. This is accounted for by the fact that a luxuriant and tenacious sod has preserved the embankments from the effect of storm and rain, and the proprietor of the domain and the patriotic citizens of the community have prevented the sacred soil from being disturbed.

The fort proper covers a space of about fourteen acres. As one stands upon the ground, the most prominent feature is the grand traverse, extending nearly parallel with the river, from the northeast extremity of the fort, a distance of 1,100 feet, to the main entrenchments at the opposite point. It was originally built 20 feet wide and 12 feet high; it has since settled about 3 feet, but otherwise still retains its original shape and proportions, and is covered with green sod. This huge embankment was built as a place of retreat, in the event of any of the outer works being taken by storm, and shorter traverses were also erected at right angles with it from the brow of the hill and the opposite side, extending southward, as a protection from a flank movement of the enemy. Five openings are to be seen in the grand traverse (four of them about twelve feet in width), which were originally covered with massive timber gates, through which the troops and the artillery passed; the one nearest the northeast end was larger than the others, having double gates opening directly onto the military road leading from the fort to Lower Sandusky (now Fremont).

Outside of the grand traverse toward the river bank, about five rods distant from this double gateway, the well which supplied the garrison with water was located. It has long since been almost entirely filled up, still, however, leaving a deep depression. The spot is marked by a white oak post extending about eight feet out of the ground. This is the end of a stick of timber sixty feet long, brought from Swanton two weeks prior to the great celebration of 1840, as a contribution from the patriotic citizens of that community toward the erection of a log cabin on the fort in honor of the hero of the hour, Gen. Harrison, who was then the Whig candidate for President. During the night after its arrival, some mischievous young men of Democratic proclivities in the neighborhood upended the stick and dropped it to the bottom of the well, defiantly planting a hickory bush in the top of it; there the timber has since remained.

At the east angle of the fort (fronting the large ravine where the British three-gun battery was planted), and extending along the north line of the fort, bordering the brow of the hill facing the British batteries across the river, the most formidable earthworks were constructed, and the solid ramparts with their bastions, curtains, etc., are well preserved, although settled materially from their original proportions. The outlines of the blockhouses and battery parapets can be traced very readily.

A line of heavy timber stockades originally extended around the entire encampment; on the north and east line, where the heaviest earthworks were erected, this stockade was placed just below the brow of the hill, and the tops of the pickets projected outward at an angle of about forty-five degrees, in the shape of a cheval-de-frise. For some distance along the brow of the bank, to the right of the west angle of the fort, there was a double row of these pickets, and the double row also continued from this point to the left until it joined the heavy earthworks to the right of the east angle, where the single row again commenced. Outside and close to the foot of the stockade on the brow of the hill, 300 sycamore barrels, sections of hollow sycamore trees, cut in lengths of five or six feet and filled with gravel and sand, were held to their places by ropes from inside. The intention was to cut these loose to be hurled down the steep bluff in the event of a storming party attempting to take the fort by assault. There were three outer gates to this stockade, for the passage of troops and teams—one, at a roadway leading down to the river from about the center of the line running along the brow of the hill, through which the garrison was, for a time, supplied with water; one, to the right of the south angle of the fort, where the forges and repair shops were located; one, to the right of the east angle, on the military road leading to Lower Sandusky. The line of these stockades can be followed, in many places, distinctly by the depressions in the ground caused by their decay : time, however, has destroyed every vestige of the stockade itself, excepting the decayed stumps under the surface.

At the southwest extremity of the fort was the main defense, constructed after the outer ramparts had all been completed (probably between the first and second sieges). After it was finished, the officers' quarters, store-houses and magazine were moved into it from the opposite end of the fort. The first and second locations of the magazines are marked by mounds, each about three feet high and twenty feet in diameter. The well defined outlines of this main defense are portrayed in the accompanying illustrations. It was in the shape of a parallelogram, the east and west lines being 230 and the north and south lines 190 feet in length, measuring from the outer corners. At each angle there were strong blockhouses which were connected together from their inner corners by a stout timber palisade. Outside of the pickets and around the blockhouses was a glacis or wall of earth about eight feet thick, sloping outward from the feet of the pickets, covered with heavy facines, extending to a ditch, originally about fifteen feet wide and eight feet deep. Near the blockhouse at the north angle of this stronghold, on the brow of the hill, was the main battery, where Harrison stood watching the movements of Dudley's men over the river.

On the parade ground, about midway between the grand traverse and the outer extremity of the fort at the brow of the hill, is the officers' burial ground. Lieut. Walker's grave was surrounded by a neat picket fence and marked by a headstone, erected to his memory by his friends; these, however, have long since disappeared, the latter having been carried off piece-meal by relic-hunters. The small tract in the south part of the fort, dedicated principally as a burial place for the "Pittsburg Blues," has been staked off and never disturbed. The field on the river's bank, southwest of the fort—the burial ground of the garrison—is still enveloped by the green sod which first covered it.

When the fort was built the timber was cut down on every side for a quarter of a mile or more, in order to prevent surprise from the Indians, and also to give unobstructed range to the cannon which defended the fort. The large, handsome trees in the pretty ravine east of the fort have all grown up since the date of the siege.

Immediately after the close of the war, the town of Orleans of the North (located on the bottom lands, between Ft. Meigs and the river) became quite an important frontier point; the town of Perrysburg was laid out by the government, however, on the elevated banks below, in 1816, and the once pretentious village of Orleans became a thing of the past; it is now known only in history, with nothing to mark the spot where it once existed. The fort was then garrisoned by forty soldiers under a lieutenant; they were withdrawn in May, 1815, and the four heavy can-

non which were there, and the military stores, were taken to
Detroit by Capt. Jacob Wilkison, in the schooner Black Snake.
Since that time, Ft. Meigs has been left to the sole care of those
who owned the estate upon which it is located.

REUNION OF VETERANS OF THE WAR OF 1812 AT FT. MEIGS.

In June, 1870, there was an excursion of veterans of the war
of 1812 to Ft. Meigs, and quite a number were in attendance.
The reception given them by the citizens of Perrysburg was gov-
erned by the most unbounded hospitality and reverence for the
old heroes, many of whom were then in the neighborhood of 80
years of age. At the head of the column which marched to the
fort was borne an old flag which had waved over the battle-
ments during the siege. It was torn and stained with the smoke
of battle, and on its lower border was inscribed in gilt letters, "2d
Com'd. 1st Squad, 3d Brigade, 1st Div., O. Militia." It was
owned by David McChesney, of Warren County, O., and was in
charge of his father-in-law, Col. Irvine, during the war. Forty-
four of the old heroes were present upon this interesting occasion,
among whom were the following: Gen. Leslie Coombs, one of
Dudley's men who successfully ran the gauntlet; Peter Navarre,
Harrison's celebrated scout; Col. Chas. S. Todd, Harrison's aid-
de-camp, and others more or less distinguished.

From these veterans, at the time of their reunion on the old
fort, was obtained much of the information contained in the
foregoing description. Unfortunately the only plan of Ft. Meigs
on file in the War Department at Washington is a sketch made
by Joseph H. Larwell, July 19, 1813 (the day prior to the opening of the second siege), which is manifestly, in part, incorrect
although reproduced and adopted by Lossing in his "Field Book
of the War of 1812-15," by Henry Howe, in his Ohio Historical
Collections, and by H. S. Knapp, in his history of the Maumee
Valley. The accompanying diagram is drawn from descriptions
given by old soldiers under Harrison, who participated in the
siege, and from an inspection of the outlines, as they still exist.

An earnest and well directed effort is being made by the
people of Northwestern Ohio, and by prominent citizens in every
portion of the State, to locate upon the site of the old fort, a

Soldiers' Memorial Home. The location, considered with a view of its hygienic and other practical qualifications, is eminently fitted for the purpose, and such a monument would be the most appropriate that could be erected to perpetuate the deeds of valor here enacted, and permanently preserve from spoilation the beautiful and sacred spot where our fathers won their laurels. In this, Ohio will be warmly joined by the substantial sympathy of the patriotic citizens of her sister States—particularly those of Kentucky, Virginia and Pennsylvania, whose noble sons lie buried there, side by side with their Ohio comrades, in unmarked graves.

THE FORT MEIGS MEMORIAL HOME.

BY EUPHINE C. TOMPKINS.

As we sit on the emerald carpet, under the whispering trees,
And gaze down the beautiful river, kissed by the lightsome breeze,
Over the grassy meadows, the wheat fields yellow and ripe,
Mellowing in the distance to a green and golden stripe,
The scene is a summer picture and I open my history book,
And the friend beside me answers, as adown the page I look:

'Yes, this is the place where Harrison with his little band of men,
Stood fire from belching British guns and hurled it back again,
And Proctor had his red coats there, drawn up in fierce array,
And bold Tecumseh's savages were allies in the fray;
Red-handed from the vine-hung banks of Raisin's bloody tide,
They thirsted for more massacre, and watched on every side
From thicket-brush, from tops of trees, to hurl the murderous shot—
And still the stubborn fortress stood— the patriots faltered not.

" 'Surrender!' came the haughty word; swift flew the answer back,
' If you capture us, Sir Briton, the victory shall not lack
The honor of a meeting, face to face, and hilt to hilt,
With your men upon the ramparts and many a heart's blood spilt.'

" Three days without cessation, the sweet May air was rife
With thunder of the cannon and moans of parting life.
Then floating down the river came staunch Kentucky men,
Twelve hundred strong—on flat boats—and hope grew strong again.
And where the bees are humming in clover white and sweet
There gallant Clay made landing with his welcome southern fleet.
And oh! what fire raked them from the mad Miami guns,
And oh! with what defiance marched up those fearless ones.

HISTORICAL SKETCH OF FT. MEIGS.

"And there swept Colonel Dudley with his dauntless, fighting band,
Keen-eyed and lion-hearted to answer the command
'Charge, bayonets!' O river, murmuring to the flowery shore;
Can you tell us just how many smote the dust to rise no more?
But the foeman fled in terror, and the patriots on their track
Thus were led into an ambush, whence there was no turning back.

"Fatal error! quick surrounded, there they yielded up their lives,
Cleft by savage battle-axes and the whetted scalping knives.
"'Stay the slaughter!' cried Tecumseh, rushing on the dreadful scene
(For that order lay one laurel on his dust, and keep it green).
Down the southern bank, Clay's soldiers charged the worsted foe again,
Spiked their guns and took their batteries, and made captives of their men.
Nine long days ere stubborn Proctor owned the whipping he had got,
Moved his camp and marched his soldiers to a safe and sheltered spot.

"What was gained? Forever after that decisive victory,
Fear of the revengeful savage faded from the old Maumee,
They had turned the name to terror all along the wooded shore:
Day and night the vigil ceased not—loaded rifle—guarded door.
Day and night the wild cry sounded, homes fell to a smoldering heap,
Wives were widowed, men were tortured, children murdered in their sleep

"Now the heavy cloud was lifted, and the wary savage foe
Shrank away from English friendship that but added to their woe,
Then there dawned for fair Miami first rays of the coming morn,
And the poor man's stumpy acres blossomed into fields of corn."

Thus ended my history lesson, and every pulse was stirred
By the beautiful scene before me and what I had read and heard.
And there on the blood-rich soil by the storied river-flow
Let us rear a memory token for seventy years ago.
O, wise Ohio statesmen! could ye do a fitter deed
Than build in strength and beauty for days of age and need
A rest for homeless soldiers who on the land and wave
Made offer of their own lives their country's life to save?
A monument of meaning from base to crowning dome,
And be its name recorded—"FORT MEIGS MEMORIAL HOME."